40 Freelancing Secrets

Get Work. Get Paid. Have Fun.

Mike Gluck

© 2017 Mike Gluck
Cover design by Greg Meadows

All rights reserved. No part of this publication may be reproduced in any manner whatsoever without written permission from the publisher, except in the case of brief quotations embodied in critical articles or reviews.

Table of Contents

INTRO 2
Can We Meet For Coffee? 3
How to Read This Book 4
Disclaimer 5
Acknowledgements 6

GET STARTED 8
1. You're ready to start freelancing sooner than you think 9
2. All you need is a laptop, health insurance and connections ... 10
3. Scared? Try it part-time. 12
4. DBA? LLC? WTF? 13

MONEY 15
5. How much should you charge? 16
6. Why you shouldn't have hourly rates 19
7. What if someone asks for a discount? 22
8. The problem with working for free 24
9. Don't get screwed, part 1 (estimates) 25
10. Don't get screwed, part 2 (approvals) 29

11. You'll get paid in 60 days. Maybe. 31
12. What to do when people owe you money 32
13. Do you take credit cards? 34
14. Pay your taxes! 35
15. Need insurance? (Hint: Yes) 37
16. Want to make more? Spend less. 39
17. Spend money to save time 40

TIME **42**
18. Track your time 43
19. Your schedule is flexible — until it's not 44
20. Enjoy wearing all the hats 45
21. Welcome to unbillable hours 46
22. Think long-term 47

WORK **50**
23. How to find work 51
24. Nag people (nicely) 56
25. Why your talent doesn't matter as much as you think 58
26. Why you shouldn't take every job 59
27. Yes, you can fire a client 60
28. Nobody to blame but yourself 61

PEOPLE **62**

29. What clients really want 63

30. People remember you — not your work 65

31. Don't work for jerks 66

32. Be the intern 67

33. Bring snacks 68

34. Accountants & lawyers will keep you out of jail . 69

35. Ready to hire someone? 71

PLACES **73**

36. Working from home? Good luck with that. 74

37. The coffee shop trap 76

38. Co-working space — the best of both worlds? ... 78

39. Ready for real office space? 80

GO **82**

40. It's OK to be scared 83

About the Author 84

INTRO

Can We Meet For Coffee?

The calls come in like clockwork.

Every month, a friend (or friend of a friend) calls and asks if we can meet for coffee. They want to quit their job and become a freelancer, but they have questions:

"How much do I charge?"

"Where do I get work?"

"How do I get paid?"

"Am I ready?"

And on and on and on.

And that's why I wrote this book: to answer the questions you have about freelancing — and the questions you don't even know you should be asking. Reading this book will teach you how to get more work, make more money and — perhaps most importantly — how to have more fun doing it.

Let's go.

How to Read This Book

Skim it. Just read the headlines. Read it cover to cover. Skip around. Dig in to the pages that apply to you, and don't worry about the ones that don't.

Whatever works for you.

Here's what you'll find in this book:
- 40 tips to help you decide if freelancing is right for you, and help you be successful as a freelancer
- Some tips include a "Pro Tip" at the end — these are extra bits of advice that typically took me years to figure out
- The tips are organized in major sections by topic: Get Started, Money, Time, Work, People, Places, Go

Disclaimer

The content in this book represents the opinions of the author, and is for general informational purposes only. If you need specific advice, please consult with an attorney, financial advisor, accountant, business advisor or other appropriate expert.

Acknowledgements

Thanks to my parents for their encouragement, my kids Ben and Zack for their inspiration, and my amazing wife, Marla, for her health insurance coverage (and her ongoing love and support, of course).

Thanks to my advance readers, including Devon, Karen, Lauren, Kevin, Kim and Julia.

Thanks to Greg for the awesome cover design.

Thanks to my fellow freelancers — especially those of you who have taken the time to give me advice through the years.

And, of course, thank you to my clients — I wouldn't be here without you.

GET STARTED

1. You're ready to start freelancing sooner than you think

There's never a perfect time to start freelancing. There's always going to be a reason why you should wait. Maybe you only have one or two clients lined up. Maybe you don't have enough money saved up. Those are all valid concerns that should make you stop and think. But they shouldn't stop you from making the jump.

Here's the thing: as a freelancer, you have to be *comfortable* with not knowing where your next paycheck is coming from, but *confident* enough to know that it will come from somewhere.

You might nod your head and say OK, sure — but take some time to really think about it. If you're not ready to accept uncertainty, you're not ready to freelance.

Once you can wrap your head around that and be OK with it, you're ready to get started.

2. All you need is a laptop, health insurance and connections

In terms of "stuff," you really don't need much to get started. Here's my must-have list:
- Health insurance
- A fast, reliable computer with plenty of storage (and a local tech support option)
- Software (for writers, consider Scrivener, OmmWriter, Google Docs and Microsoft Word)
- A professional email address (not MikeDude385@aol.com)
- A backup system for your computer and files — I recommend having a hard drive backup as well as a cloud-based backup
- A solid network of people (which we'll talk about in a later chapter)

And here's a list of things that are nice to have, but not necessary to get started:
- A comfortable chair if you're working from home (I still regret not splurging for an Aeron when I started)
- Good headphones or speakers (think about noise-canceling headphones if you're working from coffee shops)
- A good bag — I love my Tom Bihn backpack

- A powerful shredder
- A good printer and scanner (or scanner app)
- A headset or speakerphone for virtual / Skype meetings
- Business cards — even if most of your work comes from word of mouth, you'll want cards to hand out at meetings, and when you meet new people
- A good attorney and accountant (more on that later)

You'll notice that "a website" isn't on the list. I went without a website for five years and did just fine. Some of the most talented people I know have a website that's been "coming soon" for 10 years. Others just use their LinkedIn page. You're probably not going to get hired by people who randomly find you online. A website won't hurt you. It's a great place to show your work, prove you're "real" and list your clients. But unless you're a freelance programmer who needs to show their online work, you probably don't need one.

Pro tip: Many freelancers come up with a name for their company, and then use this name on business cards and other materials. Having a name for your company can help you seem more professional, and may help with legal and accounting issues in the future (ask your attorney or accountant). And you should definitely have a separate business name if you're going to hire people. But you don't always need one. In fact, if the company is just you, having another name is often just confusing to clients.

3. Scared? Try it part-time.

If you already have a full-time job and you're nervous about quitting to be a freelancer — or if you just want to ease into it — think about doing freelance work part-time.

As a part-time freelancer, you can work another job to make more money and get benefits. That's how I got started — and it was great for a while — except that you can't devote all of your time and energy to your freelancing work. As a part-time freelancer:

- You won't always be available for meetings or phone calls with clients
- You may be hesitant to invest in the right tools and equipment
- If you have another job, your boss may question your commitment to the company (if freelancing is even allowed)

I've freelanced part-time and full-time, and I usually recommend going full-time if you can. It forces you to focus on your business and make it work.

That said, if you want to freelance part-time and then do something else — whether it's watch your kids, take care of a parent or just have more time to yourself — good for you. Just know about some of the limitations of part-time freelancing going in.

4. DBA? LLC? WTF?

As a freelancer, you're running a business. And as a business, there may be legal requirements you have to follow.

You should start by figuring out what type of business you want to be from a legal / corporate standpoint. You can be a DBA ("doing business as"), an LLC ("limited liability company"), an S Corp, and probably a bunch of others.

What type of business you are could affect everything from how much you pay in taxes, to your liability if you're in a car accident on the way to a client meeting.

At some point — preferably sooner rather than later — talk with your lawyer and your accountant about the different types of corporate structures. They'll tell you which structure is best for you. It may cost you a few hundred dollars to get their advice and do the paperwork, but doing it now can save you some major headaches later.

MONEY

5. How much should you charge?

There is no magic formula. I can't tell you exactly what you should charge. But I can tell you what you can base your fees on:

- Your experience level — including how many years you have in the business, and if you have any special expertise in the client's area
- Your skill — how good are you at what you do?
- Supply and demand — if there aren't a lot of people who do what you do, you can charge more for it
- Reliability — people will pay more for someone who always gets the job done
- Your relationships — if you're easy to work with and likable, more people will want to work with you
- Speed — if somebody wants a job done in two days instead of a week, you may be able to charge them more for it

So, while I can't give you an exact number, here's a good place to start — think about how much you want to earn in a year and divide it by 240 (there are roughly 260 workdays in a year, but you need to subtract some for vacations, sick time and personal days). The result is a rough idea of how much you need to bill per workday.

For example, let's say you want to earn $50,000. Divided by 240, you get $208 per day.

But remember — when you're calculating how much you want to earn, you may also be paying more taxes, not to mention paying for your own benefits, equipment, office supplies, etc. as a freelancer. Typically, you need to bring in approximately 40% more than you do as a salaried employee just to have your freelance salary equal your salary from an employer. So if you made $50,000 in your last full-time job, you'll want to earn $70,000 as a freelancer just to end up with the same amount in your bank account after taxes, benefits, etc.

Now, if you go back to the number of workdays (240), and divide that into $70,000, you get $292 per day. And this doesn't even account for unbillable hours, which we'll talk about later.

(Side note: Don't go into detail about these things with your clients. They don't care that you have to pay for health insurance and benefits. They just want someone to do the work.)

Don't be discouraged if you're having trouble figuring out how much to charge. I woefully undercharged for my first few months — I probably could have made more money working behind the counter at Starbucks than being a freelance writer. Even now, I still don't always get it right. Some jobs you're going to under-estimate, and some jobs you'll over-estimate. Over time, you'll get a better sense of what a job will really take — but there will always be some surprises.

6. Why you shouldn't have hourly rates

When you talk about how much to charge, really there are two parts of that question:

A. How much should you charge? (Which we just talked about.)
B. How should you charge?

Think of it this way — a client asks you to do a job, and you figure you should charge $1,000 for it. That's focusing on the first part — how much to charge.

The second part of it is figuring out how you're going to charge. There are a few different approaches:

Hourly Billing

You tell the client the job will take you 20 hours, and that you charge $50 an hour, so the total will be $1,000. This is fairly straightforward, and it's how many clients expect to be billed.

The problem is that it makes it very easy for a client to compare different people. If you charge $50 an hour, if someone else charges $45 an hour you may not get as many jobs. (Yes, savvy clients will look at the quality of your work, your speed and other factors — but you can't always count on that.)

Some clients will insist on hourly billing, especially if that's how their industry works. I typically avoid hourly billing, except for large, ongoing projects that may change along the way in terms of the scope.

Project Billing

You tell the client that the job will cost them $1,000, without explaining how long it will take you. This is my preferred way of estimating and billing, because it eliminates that direct hourly comparison to other freelancers, it opens the door to a larger conversation about the value of what I do, and it seems to make clients more comfortable.

Project billing is like going to an all-inclusive resort — you know exactly what you're going to get, exactly how much you're going to pay, and you don't have to worry about it. Clients don't ask me how many hours I've spent on a project, because they don't care — all they know is that they're going to be charged the flat fee.

Value Billing

You figure out what the job is worth to the client and charge accordingly. For example, you might tell a local pizzeria that you can build their website for $10,000 — and tell a national pizza chain that the same exact website will cost them $40,000. Why? Because even though it's the same amount of work, the value of the work is much greater to the national pizza chain; they have more stores and more customers and the website will help them earn a lot more money.

Value billing isn't something I typically do, partly out of philosophical reasons, and partly for business reasons — I don't want one client finding out they paid twice as much as another client for the same work. That said, value billing is quite common in certain industries, including with photographers or musicians.

The bottom line is that there isn't a right or wrong way to bill. Figure out what's right for you, your business and your clients, and remember that you can always change it based on the client or project.

7. What if someone asks for a discount?

First of all, I don't typically recommend giving discounts unless it's a project you really want to work on, and the client simply can't afford you otherwise. It sets a bad precedent, and tells people you're not really worth what you say you are.

That said, if you do decide to charge less for a job — for whatever reason — don't ever talk about a lower rate, or show a lower rate on your estimate or invoice.

Instead, always show your full rate. This lets everyone know the true value of the work that you're delivering. Plus, if the client wants to hire you again — or refer you to their colleagues — you've set their expectations in terms of what you're worth.

Here's what you should do if you agree to give a discount:

1. Show your full rate
2. Show them the discount, but NOT as a discounted hourly rate

For example, let's say your rate is $100/hour:

Wrong

- Write 20-page website about green tea: 20 hours at $100/hour
- Discounted to $80/hour
- Total: $1,600

Right

- Write 20-page website about green tea: 20 hours at $100/hour
- Total: $2,000
- Discount: $400
- Revised Total: $1,600

A word of caution: you may be tempted to trade your services with other freelancers or businesses. For example, if you're a photographer and a friend is a designer, you might offer to take professional photos for your friend, in exchange for her designing your business cards. While people do this all the time, you should check with your accountant, since (technically) you may have to report this as income on your taxes.

8. The problem with working for free

"If you can just do this one project for free, I'll have a ton of paid work for you down the road."

It's a trap. Don't fall for it. Because once you've established that you're willing to work for free, that's what that client is going to expect in the future.

Unless you're talking about a blood relative or your closest childhood friend, there's a good chance that the client is just trying to screw you over. Don't feel bad about saying no. They'll just move on to someone else who will say yes.

If a client isn't willing to pay you what you're worth now, why would they be willing to pay you what you're worth later?

The same thing goes for discounted work. "If you can help me out and do this job for half the price, I'll have paid work for you next month." Don't believe it. If it's a long-time client who's treated you well in the past, you can certainly cut them some slack. But if it's a new client, take my advice and run.

Pro tip: Working for "exposure" is just another way of someone asking you to work for free, supposedly in exchange for getting your name out there. Most of the time, people offering "exposure" just want someone (anyone) who will work for free. They don't care about quality, and they don't care about you.

9. Don't get screwed, part 1 (estimates)

Every job starts with an estimate. An estimate is simply a description of what you'll do and how much you'll charge for it. It can be as detailed as needed, depending on the job and the client (and, importantly, your comfort level with the client). I've done estimates that were just one sentence sent by email (for clients I've worked with extensively), and I've done three-page single-spaced PDFs (for large jobs for new clients).

The approved estimate will determine how much you can charge for your work. If you underestimate the amount of time a project will take, you're going to have a hard time justifying a higher price to the client later. Writing a solid, thoughtful estimate takes more time than you think — but I guarantee it will save you headaches later.

When you're writing a detailed estimate, you should typically include:

- Your company's name and contact information.
- Who the job is for — make sure your invoice includes the organization's name (not just the name of the person you're working with).
- A description of the job — be detailed enough so everyone understands exactly what you're going to do.

- The timing — when will the work start, when will it end, and are there any milestones along the way?
- Revisions — if revisions are needed or expected, make sure you include them in your estimate.
- How much you're going to charge the client — you might give them a specific cost, or a specific cost plus or minus 10% (to account for changes in the job), or a ballpark range if there's even more uncertainty in the scope of the work.
- How you're going to charge the client — is it hourly or project-based?
- Outside costs — will you have to pay for anything else (food, travel, etc.) or anyone else (a photographer, proofreader, etc.) as part of the job? If so, are you going to pay for these things up front and then get reimbursed by the client? Does the client pay for them directly? If you're paying for them and then getting reimbursed, do you mark up these costs (add onto them to cover your time and make more money), or do you just pass them along as is?
- Invoice dates — will you bill it all at once, or a percentage every month until the work is done (aka, progress billing)? Will you be billing them anything before you start (some freelancers charge up to 50% up front just to lock in a job)?

- When payment is due — is the final payment due when you deliver a final file, or when the client approves the work? Will they have to pay you upon receipt of your invoice, or will they have 30 or 60 days (or more) to pay?
- Late fees — will you charge them a penalty (either a flat fee or monthly interest) if they're late paying you?
- How they can pay — if you only accept checks (and not credit cards), that should be stated on your invoice, along with the address they should send the checks to.
- Kill fees — what happens if the client cancels the job in the middle of it? Do they owe you for the work you've done to date? Or for the entire project?
- Sales tax — will the client be paying for tax on part or all of the job? Do NOT ignore this. Check with your accountant, and know the laws in your area about collecting taxes for the type of work you provide.
- Proofreading — if you're responsible for the final product, think about who will proofread it (and who pays for that); I typically put a line in my estimates that the client is ultimately responsible for proofreading all work.

The hardest part of writing an estimate — in my opinion — is figuring out how much to charge them. What I'll typically do is think about how long the job is going to take me to do. You really want to think through every step of it, from your first phone calls with the client, through input meetings, research, more meetings, doing the work, making any revisions, etc.

When you list out everything you need to do from start to finish — and all the time it will take you — you can usually get a fairly accurate idea of how much you should charge. (You'll also have the steps listed out in case the client questions why you're charging so much.)

Even the best estimate can't address all the potential problems. If someone wants to screw you over, they'll find a way to do it. The good news is, most people aren't jerks. Trust your gut, make the estimate as detailed as you think it needs to be for your client, and go from there.

Pro tip: The more time you spend on your estimate, the easier it is to invoice clients. An invoice is simply the document you send to clients letting them know what they owe you.

10. Don't get screwed, part 2 (approvals)

Once you and your client agree on the estimate, you need to have them approve it.

The best way is to have them sign a hard copy of it. You can also have them send you an email approving it. Then you have a paper trail (or at least an email trail), and if there's ever a problem you can go back to them — or their boss, or even a judge — and show that they approved the estimate. (If you're worried about not getting paid, check with your lawyer on the best way to get approvals that will hold up in court.)

Do NOT settle for verbal approval of an estimate, unless it's from your Mom or someone else who you know and trust 100%.

And do not start the work until the estimate is approved — especially for a new client. They might tell you it's being held up by their boss or the purchasing department, but then what happens if they change the terms of the estimate once you've started the work? That just puts everyone in an awkward position.

Finally, just because someone signs an estimate doesn't mean they're authorized to sign it. If you're dealing with the owner of a company, you're probably OK. But if you have any doubts about whether the person you're dealing with has purchasing authority, you may want to ask them ("Hey, does anyone else in your company need to sign this?"), or check with the company's purchasing office. It's a tough conversation to have up front, but it's much better than having it at the end of the project, when there's a disagreement about whether or not you were truly authorized to do the work.

11. You'll get paid in 60 days. Maybe.

Here's a typical scenario for a freelancer:
- You start a project in August
- You work all of August, and send the client an invoice on September 1st
- The client has 30 days to pay
- You get a check on October 1st

So remember that work you did the first week in August? You're not getting paid for that until nearly two months later. And that's a good-case scenario. There are times when I get paid three months, four months or longer after a job is completed.

You can avoid some of this by having clients pay you part of your fee up front. Many of my freelancer friends require 50% before starting a job, which gives them added security (and cash flow). At the very least, I strongly recommend billing for work each month or when you hit specific milestones (progress billing). But the reality is that — as a freelancer — you're not usually going to get a nice, regular paycheck every two weeks. Plan accordingly. It helps to have money in the bank to start. You can also apply at your bank for a line of credit, which can help you cover expenses (including your salary) when clients are slow to pay you.

12. What to do when people owe you money

So what happens when the deadline for payment comes and goes, and you still haven't been paid?

First of all, don't panic. With large organizations especially, it may take them time to process your check. Even if you said "net 30" on your invoice (which means they have 30 days to pay you), some companies have a policy of paying net 60 or even net 90. If you're working for a government organization or large company, there may be additional levels of approval.

When one of my clients is past due with payment, here's what I typically do:

- Let it go for a week or two; sometimes the mail is slow, or someone just forgot.
- After a week or two, give them a nudge (usually via email) — I'll say something like, "I'm just checking because I haven't received payment for my last invoice — I'm assuming it was just misplaced — would you like me to resend it?" This assumes that it was an innocent mistake, which it often is.

- If I start to get the runaround from clients, or they're not returning my emails, then I'll get increasingly more firm and direct with my communications, and start cc'ing other people in the company; remember to refer back to the estimate that they approved, and remind them of any late fees that were listed on the estimate.
- If that still doesn't work, I'll have my attorney send a letter.

You don't want to be a jerk about it — and doing so can be counterproductive if you want to work with them in the future (or get referrals from them). But if they don't pay you on time, you may not want to work with them, either.

Don't feel bad about wanting to get paid. Remember, your clients probably get a paycheck every two weeks. They don't have to nag anyone to get paid. If they approved an estimate and you delivered the work, then you should get paid, regardless of what else is happening with their business.

Pro tip: If a client owes you money but asks you to keep doing work for them, be very careful. The more they owe you and the longer past due it is, the more likely it may be that the client is in financial trouble, which means you might never get paid.

13. Do you take credit cards?

Over the years, I've had half a dozen clients ask if they can pay me with a credit card, instead of writing a check (which is how most clients pay).

If someone pays you with a check, all you have to do is take it to the bank and deposit or cash it.

If someone wants to pay you with a credit card, you need a way to accept those — typically online through your accounting software, or perhaps with a card reader that plugs into your smartphone or tablet.

Taking credit cards is good for your business because it's convenient for clients, and you may get paid sooner. It also eliminates some excuses for clients (e.g., "The check is in the mail.").

Just remember that there's a cost to taking credit cards, and you're the one who pays it. When you accept a card, you pay a fee for each transaction; in my experience, it's typically 3% - 5% of the total. So if I invoice someone for $1,000 and they pay with a credit card, I lose $30 - $50 in transaction fees.

If you're going to take credit cards on a regular basis, it's worth doing some research to figure out the most cost-efficient way to do so. But for most of the freelancers I know, it's such a small part of their business (if they take them at all) that it's not worth the time. Talk with your accountant to figure out the best solution for you.

14. Pay your taxes!

Just because you get paid $1,000 for a job doesn't mean you get to keep all of that money. You still have to pay taxes as a freelancer — maybe even more than you paid before. And you can't wait and just pay them once a year, like you might with your personal taxes.

To deal with taxes, many freelancers make estimated tax payments each quarter (every three months). If you want to take this approach, my advice is to set up a separate bank account, and every time you get paid, put 25% into this separate account. That way, you'll have money set aside to pay your taxes each quarter.

Another option is to use a payroll company, and have them send you paychecks on a regular basis. When you do this, the payroll company automatically takes your tax payments out of each paycheck, just like an employer would. You just have to make sure you have enough money in your checking account to cover your take-home pay plus whatever taxes they'll take out. Yes, this service will cost you a fee, but you're paying for peace of mind.

If you have a spouse who works for someone else, you may be able to estimate the amount that you would pay in taxes as a freelancer, and then have it deducted from *their* paycheck over the course of the year.

There are pros and cons to each approach, and it gets even more complicated if you have other people working for you. If you want to avoid some hefty fines from the IRS, I highly recommend talking with your accountant about the best way for you to pay taxes.

15. Need insurance? (Hint: Yes)

One of the biggest obstacles for freelancers is often getting health insurance. I have a friend who's a full-time freelancer, and his monthly premium for his family's health insurance is more than his mortgage. Personally, I get health insurance through my wife's job, but it doesn't cover dental — which means I spend more than $1,000 a year on dental insurance for our family (and even that doesn't cover things like braces).

If you need health insurance:
- Talk to your spouse or partner about what they have available.
- See if you can go through your parents' insurance.
- Check out the local chambers of commerce; call around to the different chambers in your area to see who has the best deal for you — typically, you don't have to be a resident of a specific town to join the chamber.

In addition to health insurance, you're also going to want to think about:
- Auto insurance — especially if you're driving to client meetings and worksites.
- Disability insurance — if you're injured and you can't work, who's going to pay your bills?

- Life insurance — what would your family do financially if you were suddenly gone, and couldn't provide income?
- Equipment and liability — what would you do if your computer was stolen an hour ago? What if all of your files and equipment were destroyed in a fire or flood? How much would you lose in downtime? A general business insurance policy might cost you a few hundred dollars a year, but may cover some of these issues.

Big disclaimer — I'm not an insurance agent or a lawyer. I'm just here to point out the things you need to be thinking about. Go talk with an expert about what's right for you.

16. Want to make more? Spend less.

Part of how much money actually ends up in your wallet depends on how much clients pay you. But a big part of it depends on how much you're spending.

In my experience, it's very easy to rack up $500 or even $1,000 a month in expenses when you add up:
- Office supplies
- Your cell phone
- Software subscriptions
- Professional fees (for your accountant and lawyer)
- Interest on a credit card or line of credit
- Coffee, food and snacks

Take the time to review your bank statement and credit card statement every month, and really look at how much you're spending — and where you can cut back.

Pro tip: Cutting your expenses may help you more than raising your income, since you have to pay tax on everything you bring in. You have to bill $125 to take home $100. But you can get that same $100 bump simply by cutting $100 from your expenses. The math isn't exact — and there are some tax advantages to having expenses — but the point stands that cutting expenses can have a significant impact.

17. Spend money to save time

I know I just told you to spend *less* money, but sometimes you need to spend more to make more.

Let's say your computer is old and slow, and takes five minutes to start up and shut down each day. Add it up and that's roughly 40 hours a year — a full work week — that you're waiting for your computer. Even if you can fill some of that time with phone calls and other tasks, that's still a lot of wasted time.

When you work for someone else, you may not care about having an extra 5-10 minutes a day to waste. It's a great time to catch up with co-workers or go get some coffee. But when you work for yourself, time is money. Anything that makes you faster, better or more efficient means extra money in your pocket.

Here are just a few of the things that will quickly pay for themselves:

- A faster computer
- Better internet speed
- An extra power cord to keep in your bag so you always have one with you
- A voice recorder app that lets you dictate notes

You should never waste money. But don't be cheap when it comes to what makes you more productive.

Pro tip: Buy in bulk. When you're at the Post Office, for example, buy a roll of 100 stamps. It will save you half a dozen trips in the future

TIME

18. Track your time

If you bill projects hourly, you should be tracking your time so you know how many hours to bill.

Even if you bill by the project or do value billing, it's still helpful to track how much time you're actually spending on a project.

First of all, tracking your time lets you see how many hours you're actually working, and make sure you're putting in enough hours to earn a decent income.

Second of all, tracking lets you see how much time a job *actually* takes you to do, versus how much time you *estimated* for it. You can then use that info for estimating similar jobs in the future.

I typically track my time down to the quarter-hour (15 minutes), which seems accurate enough without going overboard. I simply write my hours down throughout the day in my paper planner, and then once every few weeks I transfer them to an online program that adds them up.

Pro tip: Tracking time can often feel like a chore, especially for creative types. Find a system that makes it as convenient and easy as possible, whether it's a notepad you keep by your desk or an app on your smartphone.

19. Your schedule is flexible — until it's not

As a freelancer, you get work by saying "yes." Which often means working to meet your client's schedule.

I'm not complaining about it — that's the business. Just know that, as a freelancer, your schedule isn't always your own, even if you're working for yourself. It's not uncommon for a client to call on Friday afternoon and need something by Monday morning.

Unfortunately, it's easy for this to get out of control and take over your life, especially at first when you're trying to establish your business. If you don't mind doing rush jobs, responding to emails at midnight and working seven days a week, this may not be an issue. But if work-life balance is important to you, think about how you're going to set boundaries for separating work time from personal time — and think about how you can make sure your clients understand and respect these boundaries.

Pro tip: Read Maker's Schedule, Manager's Schedule by Paul Graham for excellent advice about budgeting your time. (http://paulgraham.com/makersschedule.html)

20. Enjoy wearing all the hats

When you're a freelancer, you're also running a business. That means you get to:
- Make the coffee
- Update your computer software
- Order ink before the printer runs out
- Review contracts (or hire a lawyer)
- Deposit checks
- Mail letters and packages
- Hire vendors and employees
- Make sure you get paid
- Do your accounting (or hire an accountant)

When you're working for someone else, you just assume that there will be pens in the supply room and a paycheck every week or two. When you're freelancing, everything is up to you. If you just want to be a designer (or writer or photographer or…), freelancing may not be for you.

Pro tip: You can always hire an administrative assistant, a bookkeeper or whoever you need to help you run your business. Ask your network (including other freelancers) for people they recommend.

21. Welcome to unbillable hours

Nobody is going to pay you to go to the bank, build your website or get your computer fixed. Nobody is going to pay you to order office supplies, respond to a new business proposal, or read this book.

All of this is unbillable time — time that you can't bill your clients for.

So what can you do?

First of all, just recognize that it's going to happen. Take pleasure in picking out your own office supplies and running errands.

Second of all, budget for it. Assume that you'll spend 20% of your time on unbillable hours — maybe more when you're just starting out and need to get everything set up.

And remember this: the more stable, long-term clients you have, the less unbillable time you'll spend chasing new business.

22. Think long-term

"If I had five hours to cut down a tree, I'd spend the first three sharpening my axe." That's a quote from Abe Lincoln, supposedly, and it's a good one. Because your job isn't always to work as quickly as possible. It's to work as efficiently and effectively as you can.

Here are a few examples:

- If you're working from home, take a full day to set up your home office. Get all the supplies you need and figure out where everything should be so you can find things quickly and easily. Yes, you're investing hours up front — but the time you save every day will add up fast.
- Spend an hour or two learning the keyboard shortcuts on your laptop and setting up bookmarks for websites you visit on a regular basis.
- When you're talking with a client about a new job, think about all the input you'll need up front, so you can avoid a dozen phone calls and emails back and forth.

As a writer, every time I start a new project, I set up a new file using Scrivener, my go-to writing software. It can take a few hours to set up and organize my Scrivener file, but after that initial set-up working in Scrivener easily makes me 10% more productive. In the long run, it's a no-brainer.

When you work for someone else, you don't always think about wasting time. But as a freelancer, you're essentially paying yourself to work. Look at the big picture, think about the best way to get the job done, and figure out how to be productive long-term — not just in the next five minutes.

TIME

WORK

23. How to find work

Work comes from people. And people won't hire you unless they know who you are, what you do and how well you do it. The more people who know that you exist, the more work you'll get. It's just a numbers game.

Your work comes from your network

As a freelancer — especially at first — you will be highly dependent on your network. These are the people you know well, including your friends, family, classmates, colleagues, neighbors, etc. (Pay special attention to current and former colleagues; they know your work, and they're probably employed in an industry that needs your skills.)

Your first job as a freelancer is to let the people in your network know that you're freelancing. Here's a sample email script:

"Joe — Hope all is well with you. I just wanted to let you know that I'm starting to freelance as of January 1. I'm not sure if you use freelancers (or know others who do), but I'd love to stop by your office for 10 minutes one day next week — at your convenience — to show you a few of my recent projects and catch up. Is there a day / time that's good for you?"

This does a few things:
- It lets them know you're freelancing
- It asks for a meeting at their office, where you may be able to meet their colleagues and grow your network
- It asks them to think about referring you to people in their network
- It doesn't put any pressure on them to hire you for a project — you're just asking for 10 minutes of their time

Whatever you do, do *not* underestimate your network. Over the past decade, 99% of my billings have come from people I know and their referrals.

That said, if you're young, new in town or just shy, you should really think about how you're going to get projects. It's probably going to be harder for you to get started as a freelancer — not because you're less talented, but simply because you don't have as many relationships with people who can give you work.

Ask for referrals

Everyone knows someone.

Your neighbor probably doesn't work in your industry. But they likely know people who do. Same for your friends, family and everyone else you know.

The people in your network may not be able to hire you, but they still want to help you. You just have to let them know how.

Here's what I typically tell people in my network:

"If you know anyone who needs a writer, please feel free to share my contact information with them. I specialize in writing websites, brochures and books about complex subjects, but I'm always happy to meet with new people and talk about what they need."

(And when you do get a referral, make sure you thank the person who referred you. Whether you send them a quick email, a handwritten note or just a $5 Starbucks gift card, people always appreciate being thanked.)

Meet new people

You don't have to be a great networker to meet new people. I hate typical "networking" events where you stand around with a beer making small talk. But you can almost always find something in common with someone else.

The best way I've found is to ask people questions about themselves (people love talking about themselves). When you get people talking, you'll quickly find some common ground — maybe you both have young kids, or you both hate driving in the city, or you both love wearing cowboy boots. At some point, you can let people know you're a freelancer — just remember your goal isn't to get work the first time you meet someone. (Imagine going on a first date and asking someone to marry you — that's just not how it works.) Your goal is simply to let people know who you are and what you do.

Finally, don't forget to follow up. Ask for their business card, and then email them in a day or two to share something related to your conversation. For example, if you bonded over how great the food was at the event, find out who the caterer was and send them a link to the caterer's website. All you're trying to do is grow your network, one person at a time.

Job boards and cold calling

What happens when you run out of people to talk to? You can try responding to ads posted on online job boards. I often recommend that creative freelancers (designers, writers, etc.) check the online job board for their local advertising club. If an ad agency is hiring someone, you might not be interested in a full-time job, but you can offer to freelance for them until they fill the position.

Cold calling people can also work, especially if you have something relevant to offer. For example, if you specialize in high-end food photography, you can try calling (or visiting) the top restaurants in town to see if they need your services. Just expect to be turned down — a lot. Again, it's a numbers game, and the odds are a lot worse when you're cold calling compared to talking with people you already know. Why? Because you're asking strangers to trust you, when they don't have a reason to trust you.

Honestly, I'd put job boards and cold calling near the bottom of your to-do list. If you're trying to get work, you're probably better off spending your time and energy connecting with the people in your network and the people in their network, rather than trying to get a response from strangers.

Pro tip: Over the years, I've made $25,000 from jobs that other freelancer writers referred to me — and I've referred at least that much out to them. Other freelancers in your field are your competition, but they should also be your friends.

24. Nag people (nicely)

Once you've let everyone know that you're freelancing, how do you stay in front of people without badgering them?

You can call or email them every week or two, letting them know that you're still looking for work. But most of the time it just makes you look desperate, and makes your contacts want to avoid you.

You can't force people to give you work. But there are ways you can make sure you're top of mind with people in your network.

- If you see an article about their industry, share it with them
- If you see one of their competitors doing something interesting, share it with them
- If you have an idea for their business, share it with them
- If they're hiring and you know someone who would be perfect for the job, share that person's info with them

The trick is to give without expecting to receive, and only contact them when you have something truly helpful to share.

Worst-case scenario, you'll feel good about helping someone else and get good karma.

Best-case scenario, you'll get new work from it. You'll get a reply that says something like, "Thanks for sending this. I was actually just going to contact you about a project we have coming up…." (This has happened to me at least half a dozen times.)

When you remind people that you're around, and show them that you care about their business, good things happen.

25. Why your talent doesn't matter as much as you think

Yes, you have to be good at what you do. If you do a crappy job, nobody is going to hire you a second time.

But being good isn't good enough.

You also have to:
- Know the right people
- Be in the right place at the right time
- Meet your deadlines
- Stay within budget
- Be nice to work with (at a minimum — being fun to work with is 10x better)
- Work around the client's schedule

I don't mean to discount the value of great work. I still feel like I need to prove myself every day, because if I don't somebody else will get the job next time. Your goal should be for people to be raving about you 10 years from now.

But know this: people don't always remember your work — but they will remember what it feels like to work with you.

26. Why you shouldn't take every job

Saying "no" is really, really hard for a lot of freelancers. When we say "yes," we get paid. But saying yes to the wrong types of work just leads to more problems.

You can turn down work because the budget is too small, the deadlines are too tight, or just because the clients are being unreasonable. That's the beauty of being a freelancer.

But you should also consider turning down work if it's just not the right fit for you. For example, I specialize in writing about complex subjects. So if somebody asks me to write about fashion, I'll say no, and politely refer them to a friend who specializes in that area. It's a better fit for the client, and it leaves my schedule open to do the type of work I'm good at (and enjoy doing) — which means I'll get more of that type of work.

If you have the freedom to say "no," use it.

27. Yes, you can fire a client

I'm not saying you should. I'm just saying that you can. Firing a client isn't fun, and it can get really messy depending on the work in progress and the agreements you have.

But if the client keeps adding more work (without raising the budget), if they're asking for impossible deadlines, or if they're not doing what they agreed to do, then consider letting them go — nicely.

Remember, you still want to protect your reputation. If you can, try to give them names of others who may be a better fit for them. Be professional but firm. And try not to say mean things about them (even if they're true).

28. Nobody to blame but yourself

One of the things I love most about being a freelancer is that I have nobody to blame but myself. Nobody makes me do anything.

If a deadline is too tight, it's my fault for agreeing to it. If the budget is too small, it's my fault for accepting it. If the client is a jerk, it's my fault for not firing them.

As a freelancer, nobody is making you do anything. It can be difficult to accept at first, because it means you don't have any excuses. But ultimately it's extremely liberating. Because even when things are bad, you can still take ownership over the decisions that got you there — and you still have the power to get yourself out of it.

(That said, if you're the type of person who likes to have someone else to blame when things go wrong, maybe freelancing isn't for you.)

PEOPLE

29. What clients really want

Your clients will say they're hiring you to write a brochure or take a photograph or build a website, or do whatever your expertise is.

That's a lie.

Yes, you probably have a skill that your clients don't have. But the bottom line is that they're hiring you so they can keep their jobs and sleep at night.

How do you help them do this?

- Do what you say you're going to do, when you're going to do it
- Meet (or beat) your deadlines — especially if you have a client who's nervous about them
- Stay within (or under) the budget
- Be ethical
- Respect confidentiality
- Don't be a jerk
- Be on time
- Bring extra printouts of your work
- Make an agenda for meetings
- Always have an extra pen

Some of these seem like little things, but they're not. All of them are important because they eliminate friction in your client's life. Every thing that you do is one less thing your clients have to worry about.

You have no idea what else is on your client's plate. Maybe their boss just yelled at them. Maybe their car broke down, or their dog died, or their kid is struggling in school.

Your clients don't have enough hours in the day to do everything they need to do. If you can help solve and eliminate problems — especially before something becomes an issue — your clients will love you.

Ask yourself, "What will make my client's life easier?" Think about the work from your client's perspective. What are the next steps? What is your client's biggest obstacle? How can you help streamline the project?

There's a huge difference between delivering what the client asks for, and giving them what they really need. Focus on the latter.

And remember: your clients care about their to-do list — not yours.

30. People remember you — not your work

If you bring candy to every meeting.
　If you always return emails within an hour.
　If you compliment your client in front of his boss.
　If you're a good listener.
　If you're fun to work with.
　These are the things that people remember, long after they forget about a specific project.

31. Don't work for jerks

Seriously. Life's too short. Yes, you can justify working for jerks because they pay you well or you need the work. But if you're not happy, it's going to show in the quality of your work — and the quality of your life.

And remember this: if you do good work for someone, they're going to refer you to their friends and colleagues, who are probably like them.

This means:
- If you work for good people, you'll get referred to other good people
- If you work for jerks, you'll get referred to other jerks

So if you don't want to work for jerks tomorrow, don't work for them today.

32. Be the intern

The best compliment I ever received was when someone thought I was an intern. Why? Because I was running around during a photo shoot getting coffee for people and carrying boxes and basically just doing whatever needed to be done.

I was 32 at the time, and a senior-level writer at an advertising agency. But I'll take "intern" any day. Because interns hustle. Interns have something to prove. Interns need to stand out. When you stand out, you get remembered. And when you get remembered, you get work.

33. Bring snacks

Here's an easy one — bring snacks with you to meetings.

Seriously.

Imagine you're a client, stuck in the office all day, dealing with emails and bosses and presentations and conference calls.

And then you show up with some brownies or cookies or fresh tortilla chips or even just a bag of mini candy bars.

You'd be surprised how far this goes, and how much people will start looking forward to meetings with you.

34. Accountants and lawyers will keep you out of jail

Professional help isn't cheap. But a good accountant and lawyer will easily save you more than they charge you.

Here's a quick example — most potential freelancers I meet with don't realize that they may be able to deduct part of their rent or mortgage, as well as part of their utilities, on their taxes. But your accountant can show you how to take advantage of this tax break, which can easily save you hundreds or even thousands of dollars ever year.

As far as lawyers go, many freelancers think they don't need one unless they have a legal problem. Wrong. One of the smartest things you can do is get advice from an attorney before you set up your company, sign a contract or agree to a job. Here's why:

- If you have a non-compete agreement from a past job, that employer can sue you
- If your freelance clients ask you to sign a non-disclosure agreement (NDA), you may be liable for leaked information
- If a client's contract includes one-sided clauses, they may be able to fire you without notice — even when you're not allowed to cancel the contract for any reason.

I've dealt with all of these issues — and many more — and I can tell you that dealing with issues proactively will cost you a fraction of what you'll pay (in time and money) if you get into a legal dispute once you're involved with a job.

If you're strapped for cash, you can do some basic research and work yourself. But having an accountant and attorney you can trust will save you countless headaches in the future.

Pro tip: To find a good accountant and lawyer, ask around. Typically, you won't want (or need) someone from a big firm. Get recommendations from your friends and family, and look for someone who works with other freelancers and small businesses in your field. You need someone who can understand your business, and someone you can trust. (Bonus points if they can explain all the complicated legal and accounting stuff in plain English.)

PEOPLE

35. Ready to hire someone?

As a freelancer, there are typically two scenarios that might make you hire someone else:
- A client asks you to do something that you don't do — for example, create a new website when you're just a writer
- You're getting too busy to keep up with all of your work

Solving the first issue is easier, since you can often just contract with another freelancer to do the work. For example, I'm a writer. So if someone hires me because they need a website, I'll write the content for the site, and then I'll contract with a freelance programmer to build the site.

The second issue is a bit trickier. When you start getting busier — and if you're good, you will — it's really, really important to ask yourself if you want to grow your business. Just because you can grow your business, doesn't mean you should. Think about it — do you love your craft (writing, designing, photography, etc.)? Or do you love managing people?

I learned this lesson the hard way, after hiring people and then realizing that I much preferred writing to being a supervisor and human resources manager. When I had employees, I easily spent 10% of my time just being "the boss" — and that was for employees who were smart and wanted to do great work.

If you still think you need employees — and you're sure you want them — take the advice that a friend of mine gave me (thanks Matt) and write down what they would be doing every hour of the workweek. If you can fill the week with billable time for that person (or at least time that frees you up to do more billable work) then yes, it might be time to hire someone. If you're struggling to figure out what they would do, you may want to wait. Don't hire people just because it makes you feel good.

Finally, think about how many people you want to hire eventually. Do you want three people working for you, or 30? Even if you just hire one person, you may need to set up a workers compensation insurance policy, write an employee manual and get a payroll service — things you may need whether you have one employee or 100.

Pro tip: If you just need someone to handle all the little tasks in your day-to-day life, consider a virtual assistant, or even an app. For example, I have an app that's tied into a transcription service. I wrote most of this book by dictating it into my phone, sending it off to be transcribed, and then editing the transcribed document. You may even want to hire someone for help with personal tasks, since every hour you spend mowing the lawn, for example, is an hour you can't spend on billable work.

PLACES

36. Working from home? Good luck with that.

Many freelancers start off working from home because it's free and easy. If you have an extra bedroom — or just some space on the kitchen table — you can set up your laptop and start working.

Pros
- Short commute
- Food, snacks and drinks available
- Set up your "office" any way you want
- Easy to go for a workout or do something else if you need a break
- Tax advantage — you may be able to write off part of your rent or mortgage, as well as utilities (ask your accountant)
- You can stock your office with what you need — files, office supplies, etc. — so they're always available
- Privacy — if you set up your Wi-Fi securely (and you trust your roommates), you shouldn't have any issues with keeping your info private and confidential

Cons
- May be difficult to have meetings in your home (if you even want people there)
- Easy to get sucked into doing chores (laundry, dishes, etc.)
- Not always quiet, depending on who you live with and their schedules
- Not as much interaction with other people (of course, this could be a good thing…)
- Harder to separate your personal and professional life
- You may not have enough space for equipment, depending on your job

Personally, I enjoy working at home because I like having long stretches of uninterrupted time, and I don't love making small talk with people. If you're fairly disciplined, you don't mind solitude and you have the space, working from home may be right for you.

Pro tip: If you don't want to use your personal address for work correspondence, consider a P.O. Box or a local business that offers a mailing address (some will even accept packages for you).

37. The coffee shop trap

As a Gold Level Starbucks card holder, I've spent more time (and money) there than I care to admit. I love going to coffee shops for a change of pace — but it's not always sunshine and rainbows.

Pros
- Good coffee and food
- Opportunities to meet other people
- Gets you out of the house — being a freelancer can be very isolating at times, so it's nice to have contact with others, even if it's just the friendly baristas

Cons
- Gets expensive ordering food and drinks
- Unsecured (and limited) Wi-Fi — even if your local coffee shop doesn't limit your Wi-Fi usage to an hour or two, theoretically, someone could steal your passwords and other information on an unsecured network, which is why I use a VPN
- When you need to use the restroom, you have to either trust that nobody will steal your stuff, or pack it up in your bag and take it with you
- Noisy and distracting (a good pair of noise-canceling headphones helps block out the crying toddlers, but won't always help if you need to make a phone call)

Working from a coffee shop is the freelancer stereotype, and you should definitely keep it as an option. Just know how you'll handle it once the caffeine buzz wears off.

Pro tip: Your friendly neighborhood library is one of the best-kept secrets for freelancers. It's a quiet place to sit and work. Nobody's going to bother you unless you're too loud. There's probably free Wi-Fi. And you may even be able to buy snacks and drinks, or at least bring your own. They're not open as early (or as late) as coffee shops, but if you want to save money, they're a great alternative.

38. Co-working space — the best of both worlds?

Unless you're in the middle of nowhere, there are probably at least one or two co-working spaces near you. These spaces can be a bit intimidating at first, like walking into a new office on your first day — but you'll usually find that the people are friendly and helpful.

Pros
- More opportunities to meet other people, share tips and collaborate on jobs — you may even get work from your new contacts
- Gets you out of the house and interacting with others
- May be space for you to store equipment and materials
- Secure Wi-Fi (ideally)
- You can go use the restroom without worrying about your stuff getting stolen (if not, find a different co-working space)
- Coffee and snacks (sometimes)

Cons

- You'll pay to rent space (although it's usually not too much)
- Can be somewhat distracting, depending on the setup
- May not be located near you (they're often in downtown areas)

If you enjoy working in an office and meeting new people, then definitely think about co-working. And understand that different co-working spaces have different vibes. Some are more social. Some are more serious. Visit all of them in your area to see which one is the best fit for you, then try it for a while to make sure it's right for you before you commit to a longer membership.

39. Ready for real office space?

No you're not.

OK, maybe if you're a lawyer or doctor or you run an art gallery, you need space.

Maybe you have five other people working for you and you can't work out of your kitchen anymore.

Maybe your clients are tired of meeting at the local coffee shop.

If you need office space, get it. But too many people (myself included) jump in before they really need it.

Having your own office space is fun. It makes you feel more like a "real" business — and that's the problem. Because it's fun to have space, some people find a way to justify the cost, which can easily be thousands of dollars each year. Don't fall for that trap. Spend some time really thinking about whether you *need* office space — or if you just *want* it.

PLACES

GO

40. It's OK to be scared

The hardest part (by far) is getting started. The first few days, weeks and months can be terrifying, waiting for clients to call. It's a huge decision to give up a steady paycheck. But it's not as hard as it seems, I promise. Honestly, my biggest regret as a freelancer is that I didn't start sooner.

So take a deep breath, and — when you're ready — just go one step at a time.

1. Read Seth Godin's essay on the lizard brain (http://sethgodin.typepad.com/seths_blog/2010/01/quieting-the-lizard-brain.html)
2. Watch a few Gary Vaynerchuk videos to get fired up
3. Get a laptop
4. Figure out your health insurance
5. Let people know you're freelancing
6. Do great work

You can do it. Yes, you'll make mistakes. Lots of mistakes. But they'll be *your* mistakes — just like every success will be *your* success.

Trust your gut. Make the jump.
Go.

About the Author

Mike Gluck is an award-winning freelance writer and author who has spent the past decade working with leading companies and organizations. As President of Gluckworks, he specializes in making complex topics easy to understand. You can learn more about Mike at www.Gluckworks.com.

Notes & Doodles

Made in the USA
Middletown, DE
04 October 2022